FOCUS ON COACHING

BREAKING THROUGH BARRIERS TO GROW YOUR BUSINESS

CURATED BY

JULIE PERSHING

FOCUS ON COACHING, BREAKING THROUGH BARRIERS TO GROW YOUR BUSINESS

Copyright © 2020 by Gallivant Press and featured authors:
    Dr. Fred Rouse
    Deb Dougal
    Julie Pershing
    Melony Buenger
    Dr. Teri Rouse
    Kirsten Klug
    Chérie Ronning
    Shana O'Brien
    Nichole Nadkarni

All rights reserved. No part of the book may be reproduced or transmitted in any form or by any means without written permission from the author.

ISBN: 978-1-947894-10-5

Printed in USA

DEDICATION

This book is dedicated to the people who have a passion and a vision to help others to succeed. We call them coaches, mentors, and teachers.

It's hard work being a coach; it takes training and dedication. You must be both strong and vulnerable. You hold people accountable, and you must model accountability and integrity.

The training, certifications, and ongoing education all come at a cost, but our coaches, mentors, and teachers put in the time and the money because they care about *our* success.

Thank you to the coaches and mentors I have personally worked with. I want to let you know I listen to you, and I work hard to implement what you teach me. There are times I fail, but you have been there to pick me up and give me new direction and hope.

Julie Pershing

Table of Contents

Introduction 1

Breaking through the Invisible Barriers that Stop Your Business Growth 5

Bring Your Joy, Raise Your Energy, Live Your Purpose 21

Your Book Map 39

God-Sized Goals 53

Hard Work+Dreams+ Dedication=Success 73

The Art Of Connecting 91

The 3 C's of Coaching 105

Do I Need a Business Coach? 115

Three Steps to Business Success 127

Introduction

The coaching industry is huge.

It has grown exponentially in the last fifty years. Coaching used to be just for athletes, but now just about every vocation has some kind of coach or mentor you can work with to "up your game."

Corporations started using coaching for goal setting and problem solving. Next came Life Coaching. We were turning to our coaches to help us navigate life decisions, advise us on career decisions, and boost our confidence.

As business and life coaching became more mainstream, the training and certification programs for professional coaches became widely recognized and sought after.

What do you look for in a business coach? Is it different than what you look for in a personal trainer? What about a singing coach or a tutor? How about a football or soccer coach? As crazy as it sounds, each one of these professions has things in common.

If you are looking for a coach, mentor, or tutor, you want someone who is an expert in their field. You'll check into their background and experience. Do they have any required certifications? How long have they been coaching? Do they have endorsements or references? Do they have a proven method or system to help you succeed? Are they professional? Do they have integrity? *Do you resonate with this person?*

When you hire a business coach, you are hiring someone to help you move your business forward or take it to the next level.

The chapters in this book are written by coaches who are experts in different disciplines, and I believe you will find something valuable from each one that you can use in your business or your life.

FOCUS ON COACHING

> If you want to accomplish more; Do Less.
>
> **DR. FRED ROUSE**

Breaking through the Invisible Barriers that Stop Your Business Growth

Why can't you get your business to grow to where you want? You're an entrepreneur or aspire to be one. Maybe you've worked for someone in the past. Maybe you work for someone now, but along the way something inside of you said you need to go out on your own.

It could have come to you all by itself or been prompted by a company downsize or unwanted move to another city.

It happens for dozens of reasons. But it happens, and it happened to you.

You don't want an ordinary business. You want one that will generate enough money to lead an iconic life. You don't need to buy a Lamborghini every other month. However, at a minimum, the business should generate the money and lifestyle to put you on the "better side of comfortable."

And now you're trying to start or build that business. You've got at least some technical skills. And you can provide a product or service of at least a reasonable, if not a superior quality at a fair price. But *the business doesn't seem to grow no matter what you do. And you do almost everything!*

You go to the business meetings for the meet-and-greet and pass out business cards. If you have a local business, you've printed and passed out flyers and paid some kids to place them on windshields at the local mall. You've tried some of that social media stuff that was supposed to guarantee your success and brand awareness. You have a website. You've posted blog content. You put together a "webinar" and paid for advertising in the local paper and or on Facebook and no one came. Or, if someone came, they left early and didn't buy.

Your funds are getting tight. Your relationships, if you're lucky enough to have any at this point, are definitely strained. You are consumed with trying to get your business off the ground and end up putting in 60–70+ hours a week trying to make it happen, ... and it doesn't.

You spend money with business coaches, branding, Facebook and YouTube ad "experts." You go through tons of emails with things and services that are going to get you tons of low or no-cost traffic. You've heard it all. "Live to grind." "No pain, no gain." And, "Burn that bridge behind so you can move forward."

This isn't what it was supposed to be. This isn't how it was supposed to go.

You're doing everything you can think of but not getting that result you want. As an entrepreneur/solopreneur you get to wear all the hats in the company: CEO, marketing manager, IT, accounting, collections, and staff, actually providing the service/product. You have lots of balls to keep in the air at any one time. And you have lots of decisions to make on a daily basis. None of which has any guarantee of success. And you feel it every day.

You may not know it, but there is an invisible barrier that prevents you from moving past where you are today, and it may not be what you think. It's one that no one wants to talk about or even acknowledge exists. And at this point in time, it affects *every* facet of your life.

It's the stress that comes from knowing that your money is tight, and you *need* to make that next sale, or you will end up putting your utility bill on your credit card this month, ... again.

It's the stress that comes from doing all those things, desperately trying to make things happen to generate sales and they're just not keeping up with the expenses, let alone generate a profit.

Now there are tons of things people do to self-treat stress; food, mindless TV, smoking, drugs, alcohol, and sex. The more mainstream methods generally involve sleep, diet, exercise, meditation, and therapy. All of these work in varying degrees at different times for different people. The one thing they all have in common is that they are attempting to work on the effects of the stress.

While we're talking about entrepreneurs/solopreneurs or anyone that's actually working, let's come to the basic realization of *why* we're doing those things. It's not for the enduring pleasure of the job or profession, even if it does provide some measure of that. It's for the money, and for the iconic lifestyle and freedom that money can buy! If we didn't do it for the money, we'd volunteer our time and not take the money at all. The actual end goal of the years of work and or building a business is, at some time, to retire or have the freedom to retire and do the things we want to do without worrying about money.

With that being said, . . . *Why don't we look at the cause of the stress and treat that?* There's one of you. You have many hats to wear, many jobs to do, with all the underlying tasks that need to be accomplished to make money and run a successful business.

Let's work in two distinct critical areas to reduce the root cause of your stress.

1. **Productivity**: Get more done in less time.
2. **Plan B**: Because Plan A may take years to accomplish.

Productivity is a time management issue

It's not attempting to do more of everything. Or even grouping activities, though that helps. There is a more basic issue to productivity that seems, on the surface, counterintuitive.

If you want to accomplish more, do less.

Every day, on top of the required "activities" you need to complete, you are presented—bombarded, actually—with "opportunities." Let us help you to ... make more money. Streamline your work. Get you more traffic or leads. Save you money. Make more money ... !

Some of these are legitimate opportunities that may actually make you money or do what they say they are going to do. However, if you investigate even half of them, that's time away from doing the few basic things you need to do to grow your business.

If you want to accomplish more, do less. Try as if your life depended on it (because your sanity and your business life *do!*) to say no. Don't take more than five seconds to decide to say no, because even at just one minute apiece you can quickly lose 30–60+ minutes a day or more looking over and reviewing things that divert you from what you need to do in and on your business.

If you want to accomplish more, do less. Cutting out all the extraneous "things" will help keep you focused on the important and *not* the "urgent" things that waste time, money, and energy.

SOS (Shiny Object Syndrome) affects most everyone at some time. For the entrepreneur/solopreneur this quickly becomes disabling and deadly.

When you increase your productivity by focusing on those important things that lead to more business and eliminate Shiny Object Syndrome you directly attack one of the main root causes of your stress.

Have a Plan B, because Plan A may take years to accomplish

If you've ever read a story, watched a movie, sat through a webinar or been through any coaching program, chances are you already know that the person who's climbed to success generally has had an arduous journey of years, with many failures along the way, before reaching that "overnight" success.

We're all grown-ups here and we mentally understand that. However, for the entrepreneur/solopreneur that simple concept never seems to be completely reconciled with the day-to-day realization that if we want to make it to the top, or somewhere close, that *we* are likely to have to go through those things too.

Not having that understanding internalized and having a way to deal with it on a daily basis when it occurs—and it occurs almost every day—is the second main root cause of stress. So how can we deal with this?

Wouldn't it be nice if, while we're going through the years of trials and tribulations that come with our Plan A, we could have a Plan B.

Simply to know that you had an operational Plan B in place would considerably, if not entirely, eliminate the stress that comes from the years of activities and the never "knowing" that what we're doing on a daily basis is going to get the result that we were making all these efforts to achieve.

Consider Jean and Rick from Riverside, California. Rick retired at age 56 with a very healthy seven-figure nest egg. He worked and his Plan A came together,... or so he thought.

He's 68 years old now. When the stock market crashed in 2008, he lost 43% of his money. He went into a full-blown panic and invested the money he had left with "friends" he had known for over twenty-five years that were very experienced in their own businesses. He ended up losing the rest of his money and only pulled it out when he was down to $1,200.

They spent the next few years downsizing and saving every penny of a small pension they had. They lived month to month. They were both pretty depressed but determined not to accept what looked like their fate. He kept searching for something. He emailed me this comment:

> *"I was watching a YouTube video when Dr. Fred appeared on the screen. I found myself absorbed with what he was saying. I now feel optimistic again, invigorated and determined to restart a fulfilling retirement. Thank you, Dr. Fred."*

This is someone who did everything right. With well over one million dollars, he got wiped out in the **first** market crash of his retirement. At 68, he'll experience at least one, possibly two more market crashes, while he's in retirement. He and Jean are both in really good health, so, *now* when those crashes happen, they'll be basically unaffected, because their cash flow will be independent of the markets, due to their new Plan B.

Then there's Billy Ray. He's 67, living in Indiana. He had his own business for a while; it crashed and burned with a bad turn of the economy. He worked various jobs over the years and while I was on a call with him, he told me he was day trading a nine-minute chart from 8:30 am to 12:30 pm every day before he did his six-hour shift at Lowe's. That meant he couldn't leave his computer screen from 8:30 in the morning until after noon every day. Every nine minutes he got a new chart on the screen and had to make constant trading decisions the entire time. He's 67. That's a lot of stress. He would have been happy making just $100–$200 per month, because most day traders lose money.

I haven't gotten him out of Lowe's yet, but we saved him twenty hours a week by quitting day trading, and he's well on his way to leaving Lowe's as well. This is what he wrote:

> "I was day trading 4 hours a day, and barely making any money, and then I went to do my six-hour shift at Lowes. Then I talked to Dr. Fred. He made all the difference and turned my life around."

What can we learn?

In both situations these folks thought they were doing everything right for their Plan A. They thought they were prepared. However, outside factors, over which they had no control, upended and basically destroyed their lives.

Building their savings to over seven figures and having their own businesses didn't work for these folks.

While they were going along and things were working out okay for them, both Rick and Jean and Billy Ray had a misplaced hope that things would just continue along that path and they'd be okay following their Plan A.

When things turned bad—and they always do at some point—they quickly realized that they didn't have any real control over their money or the economy in general and that

Plan A was no longer going to work.

So, what do we do while we're working on our Plan A? To reduce or eliminate completely the stress that's holding back the growth of your Plan A: have a Plan B!

What should a Plan B look like?

Your Plan B needs some very basic elements. It should:

1. Be easy to learn;
2. Be simple to start and use;
3. Not tie up tons of capital;
4. Not tie up tons of time on a daily basis;
5. Be proven (to yourself!) to work;
6. Make enough money that if things go completely awry with Plan A, it will be comfortable for an extended time.

Your Plan B should do all that. It's there to let you know that when you have problems with your Plan A, there is no need to stress. Yes, there will be problems. It's part of the learning experience as we move through things.

Your Plan B is the cheapest insurance policy you'll ever get. And it's one you have complete control over, so you can sleep well, knowing

PRO TIP

Once your Plan B is in place, you always know that no matter how bad things get, you're protected.

that you'll always have, at a minimum, a better-than-average lifestyle if not an actual iconic life.

How do you create a Plan B?

I've been working with select individuals and small businesses with 0-6 employees for over thirty years and noticed that every one of them has this same problem.

They generally know where they are financially. They know the spot they want and need to end up in, their Ultimate Secure Retirement.

They know their current lifestyle of working and trying to perfect their Plan A has them stressed and they're not 100% sure they'll ever be able to retire to the lifestyle they once dreamed of. They have a very difficult time finding where all the pieces fit together, how to stay focused on what's important long term, and how to get that iconic lifestyle along with the money and time to enjoy it.

I developed The REAL Money Doctor's "Iconic Life Action Guide."

It covers what you need to develop for your Plan B move to the next level of your journey as you work on your Plan A. It shows you how to get to get and stay focused on the things that matter most to you.

This is an invaluable resource to help you locate exactly where you're at and the steps needed to move you closer to your stress free Ultimate Secure Retirement.

FOCUS ON COACHING

Because you obviously have an interest in securing your retirement by reading this section of this book, I'd like to offer you this invaluable guide, the "Iconic Life Action Guide" at no cost.

To download your free copy, go to:

DrRouseNow.com/iconiclife

LEARN MORE ABOUT...

Dr. Fred Rouse

Dr Fred Rouse, CFP (aka The REAL Money Doctor) has been helping select individuals and small business owners with 0-6 employees for over thirty years by showing them how to structure their companies and personal finances for the maximum control, privacy and tax savings.

Today, his passion is to help people get, protect and enjoy their money, life and retirement. He developed a unique program after ten years of research and testing called Short Window Retirement Planning. In it, he shows people how they can retire in the next 3-5 years starting with as little as $10,000.

Dr Rouse is a national award winning, three time bestselling author, writing with Jack Canfield and Brian Tracy.

He has been quoted in the Wall Street Journal, Forbes, Newsweek, Inc Magazine and USA Today. Dr Rouse's work has been seen multiple times on ABC, NBC, CBS, CNBC, Fox News, Bravo A&E and more.

www.DrFredRouse.com

FOCUS ON COACHING

> "What high performance habit will you start to practice today?"
>
> **DEB DOUGAL**

Bring Your Joy, Raise Your Energy, Live Your Purpose

High performance, peak performance, high achievement, etc. All the same thing, right? Maybe ... not. As a Certified High Performance Coach™, I'll share the basics of the High-Performance Coaching process.

The High Performance Institute defines High Performance as "succeeding beyond standard norms consistently over the long-term, while maintaining positive relationships and health."

High Performance Living is described as "the ongoing

feeling of full engagement, joy and confidence that comes from living from your best self."

Those habits and routines that help us be our "best self" at a high performance level is consciously chosen, performed intentionally, and continually practiced as the demands of life change. This all sounds pretty technical and a little stiff to me when I try to explain it, so I like to look at it this way: high performance habits and routines keep us on track and help us generate the positive, healthy energy and enthusiasm we need to do what really matters to us every day. A big goal is to make common sense become common practice.

We all know that we can do a quick search and come up with at least a million suggestions on ways to feel great, get more done, be happy, reduce stress, "eat right," etc. Everyone has their success story and will tell you, "If I can do it, anyone can do it!" Another big maybe.

I don't question anyone's sincerity or truthfulness, because their experience is their experience. I do know with certainty that there is no one "perfect" solution, no one complete methodology, and no one coach that is right for everyone.

I have tried to imitate and copy and follow with exactness what I thought was going to fix it "for real this time" and not get the result I was expecting.

Part of my coach training framework is to allow myself

and my clients to trust the process and discover their own solutions. It is truly a process, and it is pretty exciting to see what happens.

I like to dance, so look at our progress like dancing. Sometimes we move forwards, sometimes take a step sideways or even backwards, and once in a while get thrown into a spin and a kick turn and dip! When our feet get stepped on or we get off the beat, it can be painful or awkward, but the music keeps playing. That's when my husband says, "Just keep smiling!"

My Life as a High Achiever

I grew up as a curious explorer. I roamed all the trails and rivers and climbed all the rocks and trees wherever I lived. However, my exuberant nature was often met with severe punishment and commands to "Do it right!" or I was yelled at and told, "Children are to be seen and not heard!"

Getting approval instead of punishment drove me to be a high achiever, so I excelled academically and in music and sports. I also had a great desire to help other people, so discovering that a music therapy major was a way to combine my musical abilities with helping others reach their goals was a perfect fit. I loved what I learned about the power of the mind to help the body.

I lived overseas for eighteen months as a missionary following graduation then got a job as a music therapist. I enjoyed dance, running long distance races, being a radio broadcaster, martial arts, community theater, and youth and community service in the small town I lived in. My friends sparked my interest in health research. But I knew there was more for me to explore and conquer.

I moved to Dallas, Texas for graduate school and soon met my sweetheart, started a small private practice, got married ten months later, and fourteen months later gave birth to my first child, all while still in school and completing my master's degree.

We started remodeling our first home, and when my daughter turned one, I resumed working in two facilities a few hours a week as a music therapist until the birth of my second child two years later.

Fast forward a few years. I remember one day clearly. My five-year-old daughter was bossing around my two-year-old son, who was taking away the toy of my one-year-old son. I looked around and all I heard and saw was noise, chaos, and mess. I was exhausted and felt I had no more patience. On top of this, I had just learned that I was pregnant with number four.

Fear and terror took hold of me, and I did the most logical thing I could think of. I went into my closet and closed the door. This was my monthly strategy. In the mid-1990s, no one talked about anxiety or depression, and I was barely aware that this was what I was experiencing.

The interesting thing was that my master's thesis was about the effects of music therapy on anxiety and depression! I knew my children were normal, healthy children, and that I was the one with the problem.

I fantasized dying in childbirth with my fourth child and having some other wonderful woman magically coming into my family's lives and replacing me, who would be so much more organized and patient and be a better mother than I thought I could ever be. My high achiever reality was gone.

I knew I couldn't stay in my closet for long, so we went on a walk, the next best choice for three preschoolers' endless energy. What happened next was truly a tender mercy. We got a couple houses down the street, and there was a mud puddle my kids started to play in, dipping in leaves and getting mud on their shoes. I sprinted back home for the camera to catch the moment of fun. As I came back and watched them being their happy, completely normal selves, a voice came to my mind that said, "You will be okay. Look at those beautiful children. You are safe, and everything will work out." I was then divinely guided and provided with resources to help me calm the fear and overwhelm, in the form of natural solutions. I have the picture I took that day in 1996 on my fridge as a permanent reminder of that life-changing moment.

Over the next two decades and during several moves all over the country, I was guided to one level after another of solutions, books, courses, and ideas to help me raise five children, remain married to my one and only husband for thirty years, and navigate the endless series of challenges and opportunities life provides.

A therapist told me that due to my Scandinavian ethnic heritage, there were brain deficiencies in my DNA, so I could probably never experience real happiness and should just go for "neutral." I guess she was not unaware of the research proving the power we have to change our brains and create whatever we truly desire. And for the record, I do experience real happiness and joy on a regular basis!

I have been a student and teacher of behavioral sciences and health for more than forty years. In my experience with health research and energy psychology, and with all my training in coaching modalities, the Certified High Performance Coaching™ model is an amazing blend of science, research and practical value.

The foundation of High Performance Coaching has six parts, which I will describe very briefly, to help you distinguish it from other coaching philosophies.

What I appreciate most about this framework is the research and science behind its effectiveness, compiled and improved on for over twenty years with coaches and clients worldwide.

The science nerd in me appreciates data and learning best practices, but even more, I appreciate the impact it has on real people living real lives.

Seek Clarity

A high-performance woman seeks clarity—she knows who she is and what is important to her. This is always the starting place. If you are unclear on your core values, about what is important and excites you about life, goals and activities will not keep you moving forward with joy and purpose for very long.

When I discovered my core values of health, freedom, personal choice, contribution, and fun, it allowed me to be clear on what to plan each day, and on the focus I bring to all my activities.

As a coach, my desire for my clients is to help them generate the health and energy they need to be free to make a joyful and powerful contribution in whatever is most important to them. My own clarity makes it easier to get out of my comfort zone, because unless I show up and take a stand for women, I can't serve them.

I feel that as women, we have been told what values and roles should be important to us. Those values and roles have probably been essential and served us well in generations past. We play different roles all throughout our lives, and the needs of the world continue to change. It is time to allow ourselves to change.

When was the last time you searched your heart to know and feel sure about what is important and excites you about life right now? How can you use your unique and divine gifts to help the world thrive instead of merely survive? Seek clarity.

> **BONUS 1: HIGH PERFORMANCE CLARITY HABIT**
>
> *Choose one word that describes you at your best, how you would like others to see you. Post this where you can see it during the day as a reminder of who you choose to be.*
>
> *Even better, set an alarm on your phone with your word as the reminder.*

Generate Energy

A high-performance woman knows how to generate energy. She cares for her body and mind by discovering the ideal combination of food, rest, movement and support unique for her needs, which creates healthy, natural, high energy. This supports her spiritual, mental, emotional, physical and underlying energetic bodies.

She has the physical energy, mental stamina and positive emotions to contribute at her best. I love providing ideas and resources to support this process.

That's one of the reasons I created "The High Vibe Tribe"

Facebook Group, where I can share ideas and tips and even recipes. I invite you to join us at:

Facebook: High Vibe Tribe

> **BONUS 2: HIGH PERFORMANCE ENERGY HABIT**
>
> *Get up every hour and do a "Body Buzz" for 2–5 minutes. Breathe, bounce on your toes, drink a healthy Beverage, take a Bathroom trip, put a nutritional snack in your Belly, walk around the Block, take a Brain Break by just meditating a minute or two.*

Raise Necessity

This is an interesting concept. A high-performance woman knows her core values and "big why" and is committed to someone or something outside of herself. Her inner values align with external demands and commitments. She shows up because her identity as a woman, mother, professional, business leader, etc. is tied to high personal standards and a commitment to excellence and service.

Different from stressful striving for "perfection," this is a confident and purposeful way of being that generates happiness and satisfaction. It is practicing specific high performance habits with regular evaluation that propels her forward and helps to sustain high motivation.

No one has more power and positive influence than "a woman on a mission." People have made that comment to me in the grocery store, but it's not quite the same thing!

BONUS 3: HIGH PERFORMANCE NECESSITY HABIT

In conjunction with the energy habit above, between activities, ask yourself "Who needs me at my best right now?" and anticipate and imagine a positive outcome.

Increase Productivity

For most of us, this seems to be at the top of the list of things we want to figure out, right? "How do I get more time and get more done?" is a question I am frequently asked, especially by women. A high-performance woman spends her time on the things that matter most. That comes with core clarity on what really is most important in any given situation. She has learned to say yes to her necessities, and no to what is not. Of course, there are habits and methods to structure and plan all of this, and part of learning is finding what works for her and her life. Having a good coach or mentor is not telling you the one "perfect" method, but helping you discover and consistently do what works best for you.

Start your day focusing on feeding your spirit, movement, hydrating, and planning. Studies show this one action can improve productivity over 30% in one week. I'd love to know how it helps you.

> **BONUS 4: HIGH PERFORMANCE PRODUCTIVITY HABIT**
>
> *Stay off email, news, social media the first hour of the day.*
>
> *"Your inbox is just a convenient storage place for other people's agendas." – Brendon Burchard, Founder, High Performance Institute.*

Develop Influence

A high-performance woman is a role model who demonstrates strong leadership and creates a positive atmosphere of support. She can persuade people to contribute and complete important projects and make major achievements. This may sound very business-like, but being a role model and creating a positive environment in the home or anywhere else starts a powerful ripple effect. I was raised to be quiet, passive and afraid, to "be seen and not heard", instead of taking a stand and being bold in doing what I know is right. I have raised my children in a much different way than I was raised, and it gives me great joy to see them creating great lives as adults.

> **BONUS 5: HIGH PERFORMANCE INFLUENCE HABIT**
>
> *Make plans to have dinner with a friend or family tonight and only focus on two things; listening and inspiring. Find out what they want and cheer them on. Sometimes, our greatest influence is listening to and cheering on those closest to us.*

Demonstrate Courage

A high-performance woman expresses her ideas, is willing to take bold and inspired action in spite of fears, and stands up for herself and others. Courage is a consistent and deliberate choice. It is said that there are only two narratives in the human story: struggle and progress. When we honor the challenges in life and meet them with the choice of courage, we progress in whatever we pursue.

In some ways, courage is the cornerstone to high performance. It takes courage to discover and stand up for your core values and then organize your life and activities around those values and what is necessary for you. It takes courage to speak up and try to influence others, to adopt better health habits, and to make any positive change.

> **BONUS 6: HIGH PERFORMANCE COURAGE HABIT**
>
> *When you are faced with a difficult conversation or action, close your eyes and imagine your most strong and confident self, standing next to you, like a strong, happy, future you.*
>
> *What would your most courageous self coach you to do? Do that.*

The great thing about developing high performance habits is that they support and strengthen each other. In coaching women, there is always forward movement and progress. I genuinely find every woman's life and experiences inspiring. To see them get clarity and claim their wholeness, understand and develop their divine gifts, and see their true beauty in action brings me great satisfaction

What high performance habit will you start to practice today?

and happiness.

My invitation to you is to bring your joy, raise your energy, and live your purpose. Whether it is with me or someone else, it is your time. I hope we get to connect sometime in one way or another.

I would love to send you a "Pillars of High Performance" worksheet. What we think about and put emphasis on is what we become. These questions are a powerful reminder of the things that matter most.

Ask yourselves these questions throughout your day to be your best self and live your purpose. Go to VibrantLifeStrategies.com to get your free copy.

LEARN MORE ABOUT...

Deb Dougal

Deb Dougal is a speaker, best selling author, and Certified High Performance Coach™. She is the founder of Vibrant Life Strategies and creator of the Vibrant Life Experience and the Vibrant Life Code.

She integrates the latest neuroscience and health research with timeless common sense principles, teaching and training groups of all ages for forty years.

Deb loves to help her clients discover and live from their core values and create lives of joy, health, confidence and contribution. She has lived all over the United States, loves travel, and has enjoyed a life-long commitment to personal growth and healthy living.

Deb loves her husband of 30 years, and is the mother of 5 amazing grown children.

Connect with Deb Dougal:
Facebook Groups: Vibrant Life Strategies, and The High Vibe Tribe
Email: Deb@VibrantLifeStrategies.com
Phone: 360.901.0454

FOCUS ON COACHING

> Maybe my story will help that one person who needs a lifeline.

JULIE PERSHING

Your Book Map

There is a story inside you. Have you thought about how and when you will share it? What do you need to propel yourself forward? There is a voice inside your head, the one *only you* can hear, and it is telling you, "I want to write a book, I have knowledge and experiences no one else has," "I have a story to share, it's important, and maybe my story will help that one person who needs a lifeline." I have good news for you, if you want to write a book—your time can be now.

In 2002, there was a survey in which 81% of the

respondents said they wanted to write a book one day. Think about this. How many people who have the desire to become an author actually write their book? It takes dedication. First, you need make a commitment you are going to write, and then you must commit to the time it takes to write the book.

As a society, we are obsessed with "instant gratification." How do we position ourselves to do something that may take weeks, months or even years to accomplish? Have you ever said to yourself, "I will write a book this year"? Did you start your book? Did you make a plan? Was there someone there to help you develop a strategy to get the book written, edited, published and launched into the world?

Whether you want to write a book to share your knowledge, teach others, build your business or leave a legacy, I invite you to say, "This is my year, and I will write my book!" Congratulations! You have just taken the first step to your goal of writing your book!

Let's begin with three things to jump start your journey to becoming a published author:

1. Believe in yourself
2. Guidance/Direction
3. Proven Strategy

Believe in Yourself

You have something no one else has—a history. Your history

is your unique story. It is your background, your past experiences, your knowledge, and your present situation. Your story can be personal, educational, inspirational or informational. Think about it, you are an expert! No one else has the intrinsic knowledge you have, no one else has the experiences that have shaped you to become who you are today.

Guidance/Direction
There are a million people with a million different ways to give you coaching, guidance and direct you to whatever they are selling at the moment. Step away from the noise. Start by thinking of what would be important to you in working with someone to write your book.

1. What kind of coaching do I need—one-on-one, group, in person, on-line?
2. Do I resonate or connect with this person?
3. Does this person have experience?
4. What makes this person stand out from others I have looked at?
5. What is their coaching style?
6. Can they help me if I get stuck?
7. What kind of program or coaching do they offer?
8. Can they help me if I'm not a writer?
9. Do they have a community or group I can connect with?

10. Do they offer an intro call or chat to see if we are a good fit?

Once you decide the kind of coaching you are looking for, connect with a coach you resonate with. You will work with this person or their company over a period of time, so make sure it is someone who shares your values and who can help you become a published author.

Proven Strategy

You want to write a book, but you don't know how. You don't know where to start, much less what comes next. What if you are not a writer, but you have something important to share, or maybe your story can make a huge difference in someone's life. You need a plan, a proven method, to finish your book—and yes, even if you're not a writer there are strategies you can use to get your book completed.

You've made the decision, found a coach (me!), and the next step is to set up a strategy for success. When you work with me, one of the first things we talk about is your commitment to writing.

You're serious about publishing a book, but are you serious about scheduling the time to write your book? There are different ways you can start a writing habit.

Commitment: Think about how you tackle other tasks in your life. If you work on a project, do you need at least an hour of time to accomplish something? Do you do it in short spurts? Do you prefer setting aside a whole day for the project? Asking those questions will help you determine a general time frame.

Are you going to commit to writing for a set time period each day or will you commit to writing a certain number of words each day? If you decided on a set time period, you'll want to make sure the time you set aside will be enough over the coming weeks and months to get your book written. If you only write for fifteen minutes per day, will that be enough? If you set a time of 3 hours per day, will it be too much?

The next step is to put it on your calendar. If you don't make the commitment on your calendar--and keep it as if it were an important appointment, you won't treat it that way and before you know it, you haven't developed a writing habit at all.

What if your style is better suited to setting up designated writing days each week? Great, block out those days on your calendar and commit to writing on those days.

If you want to set a word count goal, try a test run. To write a book with 30,000 words, writing 1,000 words per day, it will take you about thirty days to write your book.

Take it one step further, set a timer when you start writing and stop it once you have 1,000 words on the page. Now you know how long you take to write 1,000 words and you can schedule the time into your calendar. When you get your 1,000 words, you can stop for the day—or if you're on a roll just keep writing!

Content: You have established your writing goal and committed to the time it will take to finish your book. Some people know exactly what they want to write about, while others have a general idea. I even know of authors who had no concrete idea what they would write about, they just knew they wanted to write a book!

What pain points do your readers have? What is your solution to those pain points? Answering those two simple questions can start the entire process!

Clarity: You know your subject, is there room to niche it down further? The more specific you are about the content in your book, the easier you can market it to the right people who want to know your message and learn how it can help them. Think of your ideal reader when you are writing and craft your message so it speaks directly to them.

You've decided to write your book, you're committed to it and you know your ideal reader. Great, but what if writing is not one of your strengths? No problem, I can work with you to get a book written, true to your message and in *your voice.*

Your Book Map®

You've just made some great strides! You believe in yourself; you're getting guidance and direction and you're developing a strategy to get your book completed. What's next? When you work with me, the next step is my signature system, *Your Book Map®*. I created this system to guide you through the steps of writing, editing, publishing, and launching your best-selling book.

Isn't it great when you know you are using a proven system to help you stay on track with your goals? You will learn how and where to start. Did you know you don't have to start your book at the beginning? I'll teach you how to create your book outline, making it easy for you to pick up at any point and start writing.

Once you write the draft of your book, the next step is editing. Don't let anyone tell you editing isn't important—it's one of the *most* important things you will do with your book! You don't want mistakes or grammar errors to distract people from your message. If your reader notices errors, they start looking for them and you've lost them as an invested reader.

Before you turn in your manuscript to your editor or publisher, *read through it!*

Send your draft to a few of your friends or colleagues and ask for input. You don't need to send it to a huge group of

PRO TIP

Read your draft aloud. It would surprise you how mistakes jump out when you read aloud. You can read it to yourself or find a friend and read it to them.

people, just a few people to make sure your message is resonating, and to let you know if they see any glaring mistakes.

After you have pre-edited your manuscript, it's ready to send to your editor or publisher. This is when everything gets real! Your manuscript will be professionally edited and returned to you for approval. Once you approve it, your book is ready for formatting. Now it will look and feel like a real book!

During the time you are writing, you can work with a designer to create the cover of your book. You can also wait until you finish the book before deciding on the cover art. If you design it early, you can tease your book launch to your audience.

I hope you are getting a feel for writing and publishing your book. Your Book Map® will guide you through the full process from idea generation to launching your book to best-seller.

There are many different ways to navigate the process of writing and publishing your book. If you want to "dip your toes in the water," you can write a chapter and be featured in a compilation book. A compilation is a group of authors who write about a common theme, and the chapters are compiled into a book. Now you have the power of many people who will share the book with their audiences. It's very cost effective and a great way to build your influence and expertise.

Maybe writing is not your strong point. We can set up a time to talk about my Done for You packages. Ghostwriting and recorded interviews can get your book published in *your voice*. It's a great way to tell your story, leave a legacy, or share your knowledge without stressing about the "writing part."

If you are looking for support and accountability, group coaching may be a good fit. My group coaching program is for you if you want accountability and weekly training.

I also have a public Facebook group, The Author Experience. A writer and author's community where you can connect, ask questions and get feedback. We do live videos and trainings where you can ask questions, get advice and meet our community.

Join the Author Experience community to receive the support you need to jump-start your journey:

Belief in yourself – We are your cheerleaders!
Guidance/Direction – Ask questions
Proven Strategies – Learn the nuts and bolts

Facebook: Author Experience

I believe in you and I can't wait to hear about your book! Let's take this journey together.

I'm ready. Are you?

LEARN MORE ABOUT...

Julie Pershing

Julie Pershing is a book writing and publishing coach, best selling author, entrepreneur and speaker.

She is passionate about helping people who want to learn how to write and publish a book.

As a writing coach, Julie helps with all aspects of book writing; from creating your book concept to writing, editing, and successfully publishing your book. She can even help non-writers publish a book in their own authentic voice through her specialized ghostwriting services.

Her signature course,"Your Book Map" will finally get your book from the idea in your head to the book in your hand.

Julie and her husband Dave live in Oregon with their two dogs, Audrey and Everly.

Are you ready to tell your story?

For your Free 30-minute consultation:
https://gallivantpress.as.me/

www.gallivantpress.com

> "One thing has remained constant, my "why" —and having a reason to chase after my goal.
>
> **MELONY BUENGER**

God-Sized Goals

We all have different goals. Goals come in all sizes, some are small—and others so big they scare us. We have different dreams or visions we would someday love to accomplish. Sometimes we chase those dreams to make them happen, while other times we make sexy excuses why we can't. It might be time, money, or even worse the belief and our mindset that we are not worthy. Maybe we go after the dream, but only get so far—and we get stuck in a repeating cycle.

Others take one step at a time and walk by faith, believing He has called us to share our passion and vision. Trying to make the dream a reality, surrendering to our calling with the desire to leave a legacy.

Wherever you may find yourself today, I can relate to you. I have set small goals I would accomplish using the S.M.A.R.T. method with no problem. Other times I have set goals so BIG that they are mind-blowing! I refer to those as my God-Sized Goals because the vision is so big. I know the only way I will achieve it is with the help of God.

Before working with a coach, I would chase my dreams and get stuck in a cycle. Having coaches in different areas of your life is helpful in creating growth, focus, and accountability.

The way out of the cycle for me was investing in myself and working with a coach. I have found investing in a coach and growing in personal development is a game-changer for my life. You don't know what you don't know.

Excuses will only get you so far until you look in a mirror and ask, "What is this doing for me, and why do I keep doing the same thing?" You may tell yourself; I don't want to be in this situation. Or even say I will do this tomorrow.

Do you find you are not keeping promises you've made to yourself? Are you avoiding the hard tasks? Maybe you procrastinate in one area of your life over and over. You might even have a habit or routine that isn't serving you and not know how to break it.

But the truth is, if you are not willing to do something

different and continue to accept your present situation, you will continue to get the same old results. That may sting a bit. It sure did for me before I committed to getting the help and coaching I needed.

Pause and ask yourself, "What am I getting from this situation if nothing changes?" If I were to get help from a coach or mentor, what do I want to learn or know? What do I need do to stop struggling and achieve success on my own? Who do I know that has done this before?

Having a coach, accountability partner or mentor can make all the difference in your current situation. Are you ready to take a big step in your business and your life? It's time for you to say "Yes!"

Congratulations on being an action taker and a dream believer! For being willing to make a change. You are ready to step up and commit to your vision. I believe we all need help along the way, if you want to get there quicker and faster!

A coach will help you with strategies. Many times, the results you are achieving on your own only take you so far. Being coached and learning from someone who has experience will save you time, money, and help with lowering your stress. Your coach will help you clarify what your next action should be. You will gain wisdom, and the "secret sauce" of what to do and what not to do. Sometimes it's a mindset thing and other times we need to take massive radical action to achieve our goals.

I have been an entrepreneur for over twenty years. I trained with top coaches and trainers, and committed the time to become certified myself.

Starting businesses and expanding existing businesses into new territory. Consulting, coaching, speaking and developing new programs. Providing training on leadership, building teams and riding the new wave of the next best thing. I have done all of these things, and listening and following God has shown the biggest rewards.

One thing has remained constant, my "why" and having a reason to chase after my goal. At first it was hard to learn to dream again and even give myself permission. I struggled with worthiness. I needed to forgive myself for past decisions because God had already forgiven me. Why was I holding myself captive in my own mind, believing lies spoken over me? I learned to stop worrying about what others think of you. They are thinking about you less than you believe they are.

I am passionate about leaving a legacy and helping others to make an impact, influence, and income. I believe we all have a God-given gift. Those things deep in our hearts that wake us up at night, won't let us sleep, or keep resurfacing in our lives are what we are designed to do!

The very thing you are thinking about right now is a God-Sized Goal, and He has a God-sized plan you are called to walk out. You may not feel ready, equipped or worthy but you are! God will equip you where He calls you and now is the time to do something. Stop asking who or why—just start doing something and being the difference-maker.

Sometimes we get comfortable where we are and don't want to make a change. Think it's too late to do anything different or put our dreams on the back burner while we take care of our children, family or loved ones. You might not think you need to do something different and are okay with your "picture-perfect" life.

I knew God was calling me to do something different, something that mattered. I started feeling like I was supposed to speak, write, share my story, and tell others about Him. This was new, and I did not feel equipped.

I grew up in the church, I am a Christian. I volunteered, served, and led in many leadership capacities. But I knew where God was calling me this time was different. I started seeking Him more and listening to where He was calling me.

God started stretching me and increasing the vision for my God-sized Goal. Honestly, I was thinking we were doing good and the work I was doing was making a difference.

But as I sat there writing my goals for the next year... the vision was becoming clearer, bigger and frankly, one I didn't think I would ever have the resources to do.

I started relying on my own understanding, man's strategies, and not God's. My God-Sized Goal was getting bigger and bigger—a goal that made me uncomfortable. You know the goals people talk about that make your knees shake, your stomach turn, and you think it would be too much. And before you know it, the "I don't know how" comes racing back. He started asking me to surrender more, trust Him bigger, and again lean not on my own understanding.

Where to start? You may find yourself in this situation. Having a vision so big you don't know where to begin. I had so many excuses when I first felt the nudge. I tried saying no, or maybe later, but God just kept nudging and making my path clear. And asking me to trust Him.

Not knowing where to begin may be your first sexy excuse. One thing remains the same, you start by taking action. Ignite the goal inside of you and start spreading the fire of your passion with others.

When you share your passion, it becomes contagious and others want to help and walk alongside you. They will refer you to a colleague, a family member or offer to be a part of your mission. It does not mean you do it alone, and the important thing is to remember from the start you are not alone. God is right there with you. He put that vision and goal inside of you.

My goal when I am working with you is to impart you with something that will serve you and move you to action! My signature system, Ignite Your God-Sized Goal, takes you through Seven Pillars to increase your faith, create clarity, and make a strategic plan.

You will learn how to create impact, build influence and generate income. I will share steps you can implement immediately to make changes in your life and in your business. I'm excited for you, and I hope this serves you and helps you on your journey.

When we work together, we start by completing the form on the next page. There are no right or wrong answers, it is designed to get you thinking and asking questions.

FOCUS ON COACHING

Answer true or false to these statements:

	TRUE	FALSE
I have an abundance of time and energy and I put God and self-care at the top of the list		
I have huge vision, unwavering belief and complete trust in God to get me there		
I own my God-given gifts and I am crystal clear on my God-Sized Goal		
I own my God Sized Goal and I know my mission		
I know the exact steps and process to achieve my goals		
I'm surrounded by people and places who support me, my creativity, and my God sized goal		
I have access to family finances, I'm owning my worth, and creating my legacy		
I'm stepping into action daily to ignite my God-Sized Goals		

You should have a clearer understanding of your starting place with your God-Sized Goal. You might say, Okay I am ready to start, I am willing, but where do I find the time for what you are asking me to do? Something you have been longing to do for years, but other things have been demanding your time and energy. After the form is complete, we jump right into the Seven Pillars, moving you to take bold action toward your goals.

Pillar 1: Your God-Sized Goal and Vision
Take a moment and write out your God-Sized Goal. Consider the "Five W's" as you write: Who, What, When, Where, and Why.

- Who do you need to support you?
- Who does it impact?
- What it does it look like, smell like, feel like?
- What resources do you need?
- What kind of team would you need?
- What is one God-given gift that might help you activate this goal?
- When are you going to start? Be specific.
- Where do you need help? Volunteers?
- Why is this your God-Sized Goal?

The goal I am inviting you to envision is not one you can achieve on your own. It should be a goal that will stretch you. This goal should be something you cannot do without your God-given gifts and without His help. You may feel it in your gut and have thought about it for years, but you've never thought it was something you could accomplish.

Another way you know you're talking about a God-Sized Goal is you may not feel valuable enough or worthy enough.

Maybe you think, "I do not have enough time or resources! How would I add one more thing to my plate? The impact to accomplish this goal is so large! How could I do that with my network, family and friends?"

These are the exact thoughts I have had when I am facing a God-Sized Goal! He is made strong in our weakness.

Your picture of this goal may take time to develop. You may only see a small piece of the goal when you begin. Once you walk by faith and take action, you may find more will be revealed to you at a later date.

It's time to get you saying yes and taking action. No more waiting for someone else, or for another year to go by. If I had learned to ask for help from the beginning when I had a God-Sized Goal, it would have been easier but it took time and growth before I was ready!

Are you ready to take action now and share your vision? Yes, I said now. You can share with someone you know, or hop on my Facebook God Squad Community page, introduce yourself and share your God Sized Goal.

Pillar 2: Serving from Overflow
We will shift from having a cup half-full to keeping a full cup for ourselves and experiencing what that looks like.

I teach you to serve from your overflow, so your energy is abundant, and your spirit is joyful. You know you can benefit from serving from your overflow if you can identify with the feeling of having a cup half-full.

You don't have energy or time. You might be saying yes to things not aligned with your mission. We address the ways we put others before ourselves, our family, our goals, and that God-given goal and His plan.

We will identify and create your family mission. You will start implementing effective ways to work from rest and serve from overflow.

You will gain access to my signature Work From Rest calendars, scheduling system and power tools that will help you reflect that glow, experiencing abundant energy and living in a spirit of joyfulness again.

This is a process and takes time to implement effectively. Working from rest is a game changer and has transformed my life.

You will focus on what fills your cup. Take a moment and think about what fills you up, rejuvenates you and brings you joy. Start with a list. For ideas to get you started, below are examples of what fills my cup:

Beach	Mountains	Exercise
Unplug	Reading	Manicure
Church	Movies	Coffee Date

Pick one thing you can do in the next seven days that will revitalize you, bring you joy, or help you relax. Write it down. Choose someone who will hold you accountable and let them know what you are planning.

This accountability thing is for Gladiators! People who want to make an impact and influence the world. Without accountability, we can be people with great intentions, but our follow-through might not be there or may only be hit-or-miss at best.

Grab your calendar and schedule activities to fill your cup. Make it a "no matter what" situation and find someone to hold you accountable.

Let me share how accountability helped me. I was taking vacations and still leading bible studies online from the Zoom platform in my tent while my children were swimming in the pool. I was going to the beach and missing sunsets with my family, because I knew I could work from anywhere and had trouble shutting it off.

By having someone to hold me accountable in those situations, when I tried to show up, they would tell me to get off Zoom, to go be with my family and abide in Him. They reminded me they had the situation covered and prayed for me.

I learned to trust our Father and my leadership team. The mission started growing because others took ownership and felt needed. My team could start using their God-given gifts and activate their calling. I learned in different ways how God would provide and equip me and the organization. God showed me how He cared for my family and the desires of my heart.

Accountability helped me learn to rest in Him and boldly walk by faith. Working from Rest and serving from your overflow allows you to surrender to God, give Him the glory and let others see what He is doing in you. That God-Sized Goal and plan are His! When we remember that His ways differ from man's ways, and abide in Him, the fruit shows up! The results are His, not ours. We can serve with joy, more energy, and less stress. *Power Verse: Hebrews 10:24-25.*

So, let's do it—full of belief, confident that we're presentable inside and out. Keep a firm grip on the promises that keep us going. He always keeps His word. Let's see how inventive we can be in encouraging love and helping, not avoiding but spurring each other on.

As I continued to share my God-Sized Goal and His plan with others, one of the hardest lessons was working on my own beliefs and His ability. I learned I would have to wait on His timing and provisions because I was not able do it alone even if I tried. Working on God's plan when He's not in it will get you nowhere. Walking by faith can open doors you could have never opened!

Pillar 3: Building Belief in Your Calling

We dive deep into the number one challenge. It is not the practical steps; it's our ability to believe fully in our vision. We need to build your faith in your vision. You will be supported and learn to be bold enough to walk in your faith and trust God to help you Ignite the plan He has given you.

Pillar 4: God-Sized Prep & Planning Guide
You are walking bolder and more confident in your faith. You will develop and gain clarity, confidence, and direction on your unique gift. You're developing a strategic step-by-step plan and walking thorough the Ignite action guide.

Pillar 5: Faith-Filled Environment
Learn to surround yourself with people who support you, your creativity, and your God-Sized Goal and plans to achieve your goal.

Pillar 6: Financial Freedom & Legacy
Many people experience a high level of struggle when it comes to finances. Own your worth and create your legacy and plan for giving. You will see your vision growing and becoming a reality now. And you are owning your God-Sized Goal.

Pillar 7: Implementation and Support Team
We focus on making your mission known, stepping into action daily with faith to Ignite your God-Sized Goal. Resulting in creating influence, income and impact in your life and your business.

I invite you to take radical action today. For each person

who has read this chapter to the end, I have a gift for you. I want to give you access to a community who love the Lord. They are excited to share their God-Sized Goals, and to support you with yours. People who will believe in you and pray for you.

Join us on Facebook in God Squad Community. Go there and introduce yourself. Share with us your God-Sized Goal. Get free coaching once a month and some free resources to help you on your journey:

<u>Facebook: God Squad Community</u>

If you are ready for more, my group coaching program, God Squad, is designed for the person who loves being in a group of leaders who collaborate, take unstoppable action, build influence, and create income.

God Squad is a place where you will reach your goals in a community of like-minded individuals who meet online on a weekly basis. You will receive live coaching to help with strategies, implementation and launches. Be a part of an exclusive global community who see you and celebrate you.

Are you saying yes to where God is calling you? Do you have a vison you want to make a reality? Are you ready to take action and ready to ignite your God-Sized Goal?

I hope that we have set your God-Sized Goal on fire and ignited a passion burning so bright inside of you it cannot be stopped. May you be so excited that you are bursting with vision and you can't keep quiet.

I challenge you to be courageous enough to share your goal with one person today and then the world. Just watch what He will do!

Know that I believe in you.

LEARN MORE ABOUT...

Melony Buenger

Melony Buenger is a certified business and success coach who will have you inspired, motivated and committed to taking action!

She is on a mission to help people produce extraordinary results. She is an expert in assisting others to develop clarity, direction, and focus.

Melony's techniques will give you the certainty you can achieve whatever your God-Size Goals are—walking by faith and believing you are unstoppable.

Her clients say she moves them forward, helping them to break through current realities to reach their goals.

Melony specializes in working with ministry leaders and entrepreneurs who want to make an impact in the world with their gifts. Melony challenges and encourages others to live with passion and purpose; to be the leaders they are called to be.

www.melonybuenger.com

FOCUS ON COACHING

> You are worthy of peace and harmony, happiness and success.
>
> **DR. TERI ROUSE**

Hard Work+Dreams+ Dedication=Success

If only success were simple. I can hear you saying it now, "I work hard, I have dreams, I am dedicated. So why am I stuck? Why is my business not up and running?"

    Let me start by asking a few questions. Are you finding that you are not getting things accomplished because there's so much stuff going on at home? Are you getting phone calls from your children's school, their coaches, and their piano teacher? Is your child bringing home test scores that are disappointing and discouraging? Does your child have behaviors that keep you from doing the things you want to do, going to the places you want to go, and those behaviors are making you and your family feel isolated and unsuccessful?

Rest assured, *you are not alone*
I will share a bit of my story with you because I predict that my story, or at least parts of my story, mirrors your own, or that of one of your family or friends.

After a failed marriage, raising a daughter as a single parent, and struggling to cover basic needs while working at a minimum wage job, I finally felt like the stars and moon were aligning. Fred and I were getting married. Kristen (my daughter) and Matthew (Fred's son) would live with us. Our blended family would have a new house and a new start. Not only this, I was starting a new job as a special education teacher. A fresh start for everyone—or so I thought. My new family and new job came with challenges that I never expected, nor was I prepared for.

The new house was a money pit. The new job was very time consuming. Kristen would come home from school and hide in her bedroom. She didn't ask friends to come over because she was embarrassed by the daily homework and behavior battles with her older stepbrother Matthew.

Matthew's new beginning included detentions and suspensions from school. His infractions included smoking on the bus, skipping class, and stealing a scale from the chemistry lab, just to name a few. Arguments about homework and chores became a daily event.

We asked the school for help along the way but the only thing they did was hand out more detentions and longer suspensions. We asked the district for a placement in a special school so he could be more closely monitored. After many meetings, lots of arguments, and buckets of tears, our request was initially denied! Eventually our request was granted, but it didn't put a dent into our problems.

Besides the struggle with Matt's academics, we struggled socially because we were often not invited to places because of Matt's behavior. And we struggled emotionally because we were constantly fighting. We felt isolated and quite honestly, we were all exhausted. We were at a crossroads and we felt like there was no place for us to turn.

The suspensions, detentions, and other disciplinary actions continued until things came to a head with Matthew. After a lengthy school suspension, Matt dropped out of school a mere three months before graduation. We were crushed. Our little family was falling apart. We felt that the system had failed him; even worse, that we had failed in our newly formed family.

After Matt dropped out, I searched for other families who had the same experiences that we did and organizations that could provide us with support, but I could not find support anywhere.

I'd like to tell you that there is a happy ending for Matt and for my family. I would like to tell you that everything came up roses and that we are all living in peace and harmony, but I can't. Matt moved away after he dropped out and we have very little contact with him now. I will tell you that I know Matt is not living his best life because he doesn't know how.

Fred, Kristen and I have worked hard to become the best family we know how to be. This doesn't mean that things have been easy, because they haven't.

We are still a work in progress, but we are a family doing the best we know how. Of course, we argue and disagree but we have learned how to communicate better with each other. We have a circle of friends and supportive family who have helped us get through all the changes. But how did we make this happen?

After Matt left, I was so angry and very frustrated with the system, with our lives and—let's face it—with Matt. I didn't want another child or family to feel the frustration, anger and despair we felt. I didn't want any child or their families to experience the struggles, the arguments, the school and financial stressors that go hand-in-hand with these behaviors. I wanted to give all children and their families the opportunity to be the best versions of themselves, both as individuals and as a united family unit.

I went back to school, worked my ass off, and earned a doctoral degree in Special Education and Positive Behavior Supports. I acquired knowledge, tools, and strategies to create our best life. I made it my mission to help other families overcome the same struggles and heartache we had experienced.

I started my company, *K I D S: Interventions & Direct Services*, which provides behavior, academic support, and strategies for children, young adults, their families, and their teachers. Unfortunately, all of this came too late to help Matt, but with all of my heart and soul I believed I could help other children and their families. I am glad that I have been persistent.

So, here are some important things I want you to remember: You and your hard work, dreams and dedication can come to fruition, but you have to make some changes individually and as a family. Everyone needs to buy in and to have a voice.

In order for your hard work, dreams and dedication to happen, you need to address the elephant in the room; the root cause of your lack of success.

Please remember: It is never too late to alter the course you and your family are currently traveling, so that you can create social, emotional and academic success, as well as create the successful business you dream of.

I know you are super busy, but in spite of limited time, it

is unnecessary to spend months or years to achieve these successes. There are three things—pillars—you can implement quickly that will have an incredible impact.

First and foremost, remember there is hope! It won't be easy, but it is so worth it.

With all of this being said, I want to share with you the three Pillars of Success that will help you *visualize* what you want, *strategize* how to make that happen, and *harmonize* to take advantage of all the great things you can bring to life for your children and your family.

Pillar 1: **Look into your Crystal Ball**. *Visualize* what you really want for you, your family and your business. You will see where you are and where you want to be—to grow both at home and in the business world. You will have challenges, but you will discover how to face those challenges and go forward fearlessly. The greatest part is that the choices are yours! You will choose when and where you will start. "Start what?" you ask. Start your transformation from stuck to productive in business, and from fractured to harmony in your family.

Pillar 2: **Trash the Tissues**. You will discover how to *strategize* and move forward to create the long-lasting positive changes you desire emotionally, socially and academically. Not only will your child go from disciplinary problems to Student of the Month, but you will have the time and energy to put into growing your business! You will discover what you want to be able to do, where you want to go, and who you want to bring along on this journey.

Pillar 3: **The Transformation**. Finally, with the transformation of your mindset and harmony in your home, you will begin the process of living your best lives as individuals and as a family. You will gain insight into all the possibilities available to you and your family, alternatives to expensive therapies and medications, great vacation opportunities, and quality time spent together. You will find different ways to communicate *and* you will discover how to celebrate everyone's successes while supporting each other when things are challenging.

Case Study: David was a fourth-grade student in a public elementary school. His parents reported that he was avoiding reading assignments. He didn't want to go to school, and he definitely didn't want to participate with his classmates. He also challenged his parents at home with regard to doing homework. He was acting out and failing miserably.

Not only was David suffering, so were his parents. Their work days were bombarded with emails and calls from school. Nobody was being productive. Nobody was being their best selves.

We all sat down and started with Pillar 1 *visualizing* what they wanted the family/school experience to look like.

Then we moved to Pillar 2 and *strategized* how to make that happen. Some things worked right away, others did not, but David and his family did not give up. After experiencing small successes, they were able to move to Pillar 3 and begin to *harmonize* as a family. There was peace in the valley!

Isn't this the same way we feel as adults when we are overwhelmed? We are trying to balance our home and possibly, trying to create or sustain our own business.

When parents discover *how* to create impactful, long-lasting, and positive behavioral changes, they begin to see changes in mindset and priorities within their families. The same basic methods can work for you in your business.

The peace and harmony you create will allow you time and affords you the energy to work through what you need to do to get unstuck in your business. It's kind of like creating a business plan with a little "Woo-Woo," so to speak.

Let me tell you *why* I want so desperately to help you with this. I know that the educational system is overtaxed and I never want parents to feel the soul crushing heartbreak and guilt of their child falling off the face of the Earth (been there, done that).

I know how difficult it is to keep home, school, and work balance. But I want you and your child to want to go to school/work, feel confident, get good grades, have clients, and laugh joyfully—to become the best version of yourselves.

Most importantly, I want you to believe that you and your children are worthy, and your business worthwhile. You all deserve peace and happiness. You all should experience social and emotional wellness, academic success, and have a productive work life.

Listen, I know that you feel you've tried everything! I get it. Where can you turn? You and your child struggle with poor academic performance, anxiety, frustration, anger, therapies, medications, ad nauseum. Right?

You have two choices. You can do nothing. Stay stuck in this cycle of isolation, poor academic performance, financial stress and emotional distress that affects both you and your business. Or, take steps to experience radical, positive, and powerful changes in your child's behavior so you can promote academic success, social and emotional wellness and a productive, balanced life.

Let me give you an example of one step you can take to social and emotional wellness and academic or business success. Start by thinking about your current state of affairs, and then think of what you want your life to look like. Please take a few moments to review and complete the worksheets on the next two pages.

Think about how you see your family now. Circle words in each row that describe your current state of affairs.

	Current State of Affairs	
Social	Isolated Lonely Left out Bullied Embarrassed Stereotyped Tantrum Helpless	Targeted Ignored Avoided Disliked Frustrated Confused Hopeless
Emotional	Tired Depressed Angry Helpless Lonely Ashamed Dislike School/Work Embarrassed Pressured Anxious Isolated Lonely Left out Bullied Stereotyped Tantrum Helpless	Frustrated Tantrum Hopeless Confused Embarrassed Bullied Stupid Alone Targeted Ignored Avoided Disliked Frustrated Hopeless

Next, circle words that describe your ideal circumstances.

	Ideal Circumstances	
Social	Included Hopeful Energized Community Invitations Sporting Events/Teams	Organized Helpful Friends Strong Connections
Emotional	Excited Focused Included Hopeful Energized Strong	Supported Calm Organized Helpful Friends
Academic/ Business	Successful Hopeful Focused Organized Energized Strong	Included Helpful Calm Supported Friends

Take a good look at the words you have identified. Hang the list somewhere you can see it as a reminder. You can do the same thing for where you are in your business.

This is the first step in visualizing what you want for you, your family and your business. Now you know what you want. You have it in front of you!

You can begin uniting your family by following the proven suggestions in the United Family Success Formula.

By the time you complete Pillar 1, you will:

- Know what you really want for you, your family and your business;
- Be able to face challenges together;
- Choose where to start your transformation from Fractured to *United* and from Stuck to *Productive*.

When you finish Pillar 2, learning how to *strategize*, you will:

- Change your mindset about yourself and your family;
- Learn how to make and keep friends;
- Balance home, school, and work.

And finally, Pillar 3 will teach how you can *harmonize*, and you will:

- Find alternatives to expensive therapies and medications;
- Experience better communication at home, with school, and in social settings;
- Feel and be empowered as individuals, as a family and as a businessperson.

When your children were born, they didn't come with an

instruction book. You probably had a dream of what your family would look and sound like. The same is probably true for your business as well. Do you want that dream? Do you want to be the best version of yourselves?

If I can offer you only one thing from this chapter, it is to remind you that you and your family are worth it! You are worthy of peace, harmony, happiness, and success. Be brave. Be bold. Go forward fearlessly!

If you want to transform your fractured and struggling family into a harmonious household living the best life you can, please reach out to me at drterirouse.com.

I would be honored to have the opportunity to get you started on the journey of transformation with the *9 Steps to Transform Your Child with Powerful Positive Behavior* program.

LEARN MORE ABOUT...

Dr. Teri Rouse

Dr. Teri Rouse is an international speaker and travels the globe every year giving presentations at various organizations including the American Horticultural Therapy Association, Division of International Special Education & Services and Educators Rising.

Dr. Teri Rouse earned her Doctorate in Education for Arcadia University. She is a Certified Autism Specialist and received her Applied Behavior Analysis (ABA) endorsement from Penn State. And she is the Managing Director of KIDS Interventions & Direct Services, UBO which provides direct services to children, their parents, and background and support for classroom teachers.

Through her own life experience, Dr. Rouse, noticed a need for families to come together. She has made it her mission to help parents take control of their child's behavior so that they can experience academic success and emotional and social wellness as a united family through How to Help Your Emotionally Troubled KID Develop Kindness, Inspiration, Determination, Success & Bring Harmony to Your Home: the 60 Day Transformation YOU can create system.

She is a member of the National Academy of Best-Selling Authors and received her QUILLY award at a red-carpet event in Hollywood for her best-selling book, *Cracking the Code to Success* that she co-authored with Brian Tracy and her husband Dr Fred.

She is married to Dr. Fred, a mother, and dog mom! She can often be found in the yard working in the garden or down at the shore with her toes in the sand

www.drterirouse.com

FOCUS ON COACHING

> A positive attitude combined with positive action is often the foundation for growth.
>
> **KRISTEN KLUG**

THE ART OF CONNECTING

"What if I can't keep holding on? What if my hand slips?" She cried in frustration.

"No, we HAVE to do this. Help will come. We are going to focus on keeping our grip strong," I followed up quickly and with a strong voice.

"I don't think I can do this. I want to give up!" she screamed as she was dangling 20 feet high from my fingertips and arms stretched out to her.

You see, a minute prior the ski chair lift was slippery when we sat down and we all slid off. I was able to pull myself and my son up, but the girl next to me, well, her hips were below the bench and I couldn't pull her up. When I realized what was happening, I jumped into coaching mode and said *"You will have to fall down 2 feet into the powder after we pass the block."* After that I was hollering *"stop the lift, stop the lift!"* The high-speed quad chairlift rushed up and suddenly I realized she had fallen, but not let go! It was at that moment; I had to act quickly and grab her.

A coach does what has to be done. A coach thinks and acts quickly. A good coach keeps their poise through all challenges, fears, frustrations, and faces what is.

In fact, this brings me to business coaching as well, as I hear many people share their fears. I have learned to lean in and ask more questions. It is through asking questions that we allow people to get more comfortable. Our conversations lead to making something tough, easier.

When the chair lift finally stopped, we were at the third pole, with no help in sight. My son was clinging onto the back of the lift and the girl and I were staring at each other. In those minutes together everything slowed down as we talked about our fear of dying, why the chair hadn't stopped, why there wasn't anyone coming to help, and a thousand creative ideas on how to solve the problem.

It was our sheer determination and my positive attitude that got us through. I stayed very present. I answered all the tough questions. And I used skills about intermittent gripping I had learned in a cycling class (years prior) to keep our hands strong enough to hold on. Intermittent grip is holding tight with the right hand and looser with the left, then switching to hold tight with the left hand and give a rest to the right. When the help finally arrived below, we had to let go and she fell down, hit the tarp and then the ground with a thud. We cried. My arms hurt and I was exhausted mentally and physically. Amazingly, she walked away, skied the rest of the day, and won the ski race the next weekend!

The reason I share this gut-wrenching story is that what saved us in this very scary situation as a ski racing coach is also what can save relationships and challenging situations in life and business.

Coaching is the ART OF CONNECTING in these five ways:

1. Be Present & Empathetic When present in the situation, you can focus and see more clearly on how to complete what is next. You can address specific needs without overwhelm or frustration.

Being empathetic as a coach gives us the ability to share our personal stories from experiences and training and really listen. There is a beautiful connection made when coaches are empathetic at the level and the learning style of the athlete, patient, client, or student.

The more we can create multi-sensory, hands-on, and/or applied learning experiences, the longer we will remember the skills.

Multi-sensory experiences are when we provide ideas that engage the five multiple senses—touch, sight, sound, taste, and smell.

Hands-on or applied learning is having the experience as you are learning it.

When I am coaching a speaker or business owner on how to take action, I coach them in multiple ways:

- **Visualization**: close eyes to imagine what it feels and looks like in the mind first.
- **Action**: act it out through all situations and questions.
- **Creation**: draw or write out the process on paper focusing on the big picture and small details.

Practicing the experience in multiple ways allows the coaching to sink in. The speaker or business owner feels more confident as they could see, feel, and touch it. They connect with their audience immediately and leave a lasting impression because of how deep they practiced it.

We are all coaches at heart. When I coach youth in sports, once they understand a concept I have them coach a partner. The more we can coach, the better we learn ourselves.

2. Choose a Creative Perspective We all have fears. The more we can be proactive in how we connect, the easier it is for us to see a new or creative perspective. Not that the fear will go away, rather it is shifting our position or mindset to face the fear and more forward with intention.

I remember when I started my business in college; I thought I needed to be located downtown and have employees to be successful. Thankfully my business coach,

Dr. Thomas Jones, said it doesn't matter where you are located, it only matters how you promote and manage your work.

In addition to promotion, innovation and improvements are essential. I have coached hundreds of business owners with creative ideas on how to market themselves. One of my favorite stories is about a third-generation farm. They wanted me to design a new logo for them so they would stand out. When I started asking questions to fully understand why they wanted a new logo, I found out that their main concern was that people weren't coming to the farm as often because of the Internet.

The development of educational materials outlining why buying from local, organic farmers is integral to our community was written and designed so they could start conversations. Our marketing not only helped their farm, it also helped local grocery stores and retailers!

In addition, we designed the idea of a Fall Festival experience so people could learn on the farm. Almost twenty years later, Liepold Farms is thriving and their Fall Festival is one of the largest in the state!

3. Keep it Simple It is so easy to make situations more complex than they are. Some of the best coaches can break down big ideas into small steps. By keeping it simple, you can make a difference, too.

As a coach I often hear complaints about people not having enough time to accomplish their vision, goals, or projects. Questions to ask: What is getting in my way? How am I setting my priorities? How can I simplify in order to get what needs to be done, done? What do I want?

In 2018, I was involved in two bad auto accidents and one skiing accident. My car was hit by a drunk driver. Six months later, I was hit by someone who was texting and driving. Then three months later, a man going the wrong direction on the ski slopes hit me and I broke my leg. I had eight surgeries, was hospitalized for three weeks, and didn't walk for nine months!

After trauma you learn to appreciate your time more than ever! Now I coach mindfulness and meditation practices in my coaching sessions in order to manifest more good and simplify how we spend our time. These practices have been outstanding for me and my coaching clients.

By keeping it simple, I hear my clients say "You give me the ability to do more of what I love." To me, this is the greatest gift of all!

4. Make Your Words Matter Your words—thoughts, ideas, notes, and stories—lead you toward what you think about and focus on. And, how you hear the words others say and process them—stories, ideas, news, and messages—can lead you forward or hold you back.

Words, in themselves, can be very powerful. They can make us laugh or cry. They can influence, manipulate, or inspire. Words have different effects on different people, and that's why word choices are so powerful.

Today, we flip from page to page, feed to feed, consuming so many words! Yet, when we find something that is entertaining or interesting, we pause and take it in. And, sometimes, we engage and share. Just think about how your words consume your time and your life.

5. Take Action with a Positive Attitude When we react in negative ways, we can go from problem to problem getting nowhere. Having a positive attitude is everything. It can help you achieve more, live longer, and inspire others.

A positive attitude combined with positive action is often the foundation for growth. Positive and negative attitudes affect your subconscious and how you talk to yourself. Our brain has a sensor in it, to first respond negatively in order to protect us. This sense is good so we don't run into a wall or burn ourselves on the stove. But in times of making choices about moving forward on an intention or holding on for dear life, we need to take note of that sensor and build a positive inner voice.

As a business owner since I was a kid, and helping hundreds of business owners and entrepreneurs succeed, I understand how our business can get in the way of life, and our lives can get in the way of business.

In order to make both more enjoyable, profitable, and more fun, I enjoy helping you overcome challenges, discover your passions, and empower you to have a career and life you love!

FOCUS ON COACHING

You might wonder, what does as a business and life empowerment and action planning coach do? I help you navigate change with more ease, overcome fears or anxieties, brainstorm your big ideas with you, discover the steps to create your dream reality, find time to exercise and eat colorful foods, and explore life in creative ways!

Currently I am seeking to work with business owners who want to grow their business through improvement, innovation, and communication. I have a creative services team to handle all branding in print, direct marketing, website, summit, click funnel, social media, copywriting, and VA (Virtual Assistant) needs. I also have a lot of experience figuring out pricing for products and programs. I enjoy creating movements and am very interested in talking with people who share a passion about whole health.

Healthy & Fun Choices® is a magazine and online educational platform I created to start conversations, inspire connections, and create community.

You and your business can be featured in the Healthy & Fun Choices® magazine to gain access to our community as an influencer. There are also opportunities for sponsorship and advertising. Connect with me and we can work together to figure out how you can take advantage of promotions and connections!

It is so beautiful to see individuals not give up! There is so much more we can accomplish when we have to stretch ourselves and discover the value we bring to others.

Four years later, the girl who held on and listened to my coaching is thriving! And I've learned how the ART OF CONNECTING brings together my passion for whole health education and life/business coaching! I look forward to the opportunity of connecting with you!

Are you ready to find out how we can work together?

- Would you like to join our community?
  Group Coaching Class - Mondays from 11-12am PST

- Do you want outstanding Creative Services? *Graphic Design, Copywriting, Market Strategy, VA (Virtual Assistant) Services*

- Do you belong to a business leader group or network community? *Empowerment Speaking for Business and Creative Leaders*

- Interested in an intensive, customized approach? *Deep-Dive Action Planning Coaching*

- Looking to increase your credibility in a shortamount of time? *Create-Your-Own-Summit Packages*

If you don't see what you need, please reach out and let's talk! I'm available to talk with you 9am-3pm M-Thursday.

LEARN MORE ABOUT...

Kirsten Klug

Kirsten Klug brings a creative perspective so people see, hear, and understand what is holding them back.

Kirsten is an Empowerment Coach for business owners and the Publisher of Healthy & Fun Choices® magazine and on-line platform.

She brings over twenty-five years experience as a business owner working with hundreds of organizations to create positive connections.

Kirsten has published eleven books, is an award-winning graphic designer and copywriter.

When Kirsten is not working, you will find her playing with her two children and husband outdoors in the mountains or lakes or coaching ski racing and soccer. You can connect with Kirsten Klug on Facebook or Instagram.

www.kirstenklug.com
www.healthyfunchoices.com

FOCUS ON COACHING

> From the big picture, to the little details, planning is key.
>
> **SHANA O'BRIEN**

The 3 C's of Coaching

When I was a little girl, my favorite game was "school." I was the oldest of three, and always the teacher. In retrospect, my love of playing school probably was more of a love of being the boss. But I didn't know how to translate that into an adult career in politics or as a CEO, so I got a degree in education. Makes sense, right? I liked to play school as a kid, so I guess I'll be a teacher.

When I graduated from college, I was ready to mold minds and change lives. One hiccup: I apparently didn't like kids that much. Don't get me wrong. I loved my own kids (still do!), and I loved some of their friends. But being put in charge of a classroom full of children that were not particularly interested in being molded or changed was quite a disappointment. I've since chalked that bachelor's degree up as one of my less-than-well-thought-out plans.

After a little research, I found that there were pretty limited job options with a degree in education that didn't involve children, so I took some graduate classes in adult training and development. That's how I learned that there ARE people out there that WANT to have their minds molded and DESIRE to have their lives changed. They're just not fourth graders, which works well for me.

I've worked in a couple of different industries, but real estate is my passion. I've built a lucrative career helping buyers and sellers make successful transactions. But my inner teacher was always just under the surface trying to peek out. My current position as a managing broker for approximately 150 agents is my perfect fit: I'm in the industry that I love; I work with people who want to learn and grow; I get to mentor and teach motivated folks who are eager to learn and grow.

Before I begin my 12-week coaching program with a new agent, we review the 3 C's required for a successful outcome. By following this formula, I have helped brand new licensees become successful real estate brokers, and I've helped good agents become high-producing great agents.

I am sharing the 3 C's because I think they can be the

foundation for building a great coaching system regardless of the industry. They set the stage for success and ensure that you and your coaching client are on the same page when it comes to expectations.

COMMITMENT Before I start working with a new coaching client, I give them a written list of my expectations for them in the program. My clients need to be receptive to new information, engaged in their own growth, and **committed to completing the assignments and exercises** that are part of the program. If they are unable to make that commitment, then my coaching will not be a good fit for them.

I also put my commitment to my clients in writing. I want them to know what they can expect of me during our time together, and I want them to feel empowered to hold me accountable. At the beginning of every 12-week coaching program, I commit to my client that their growth and improvement is my top priority in this relationship

PRO TIP

My clients leave each coaching session with an assignment. The day before our next session, I send a reminder text regarding our upcoming meeting. In that text, I also ask if they've completed their assignment from last week. If they haven't done the assignment, I reschedule the session. We can't move forward if they will not hold up their end of the commitment.

and that any question they have is valuable and will be treated respectfully. My goal is to create a safe space where there's no such thing as a "dumb question."

CONSISTENCY Being consistent is an absolute necessity for client success. The expectation is set that they will consistently show up prepared and ready to do the work, each and every time we get together.

It's a crucial habit to build for business success and my clients have to be willing to put that effort in if they want to see results.

We practice consistency not only in our work habits but in the message we want to deliver in our marketing and branding.

We practice consistency in the quality of our work product, making sure that every contract is handled equally well as the next. And we practice consistency in maintaining our level of professionalism throughout every transaction.

CALENDARING When we create strong systems, we take the guesswork out of the daily routine.

A commitment to intentional activity is an absolute necessity. My clients learn and practice time management and time-blocking techniques as part of our coaching program and create the strong habit of calendaring as part of their daily routine. If you don't make a plan to do it, it generally doesn't get done.

I start with the big picture, a one-year calendar, and

together we flip through the upcoming year setting a goal, a commitment to an action, or a theme for every month. If we know in February that November will be a month dedicated to client appreciation, it gives us time to plan, prepare, and execute.

From the big picture, to the little details, planning is key. As part of our calendaring exercise, I also work with each client on a 'perfect day' schedule that includes concrete action items to be executed daily to work toward their goals. It can't be stressed enough times: if you don't make a plan to do it, it rarely gets done.

With the 3 C's as the foundation of the coaching program, I'm able to layer in the nuts and bolts of the real estate industry as we move through the curriculum.

By instituting a similar approach, you are building a solid framework to support whatever theories, steps, or programs you are teaching.

Every time we as coaches take on a new client, it's our honor and privilege to get the opportunity to work with them as they achieve their goals. I feel that making the expectations crystal clear from day one creates an environment of respect and accountability.

And honestly, it is also a self-preservation technique. There is nothing more frustrating (for me) than sitting down with an agent who wants to "move on to the next thing" without having finished the last thing.

FOCUS ON COACHING

My approach and my techniques have evolved quite a bit from my days of playing school and bossing my siblings and neighbors around. But at heart, I'm still a teacher, and I find coaching to be the most rewarding aspect of my career. You may have heard the saying, "Those who can't do, teach." And maybe there's some validity to that. But I prefer to see it as, "Those who can do, share." Systemizing my formula for success and then sharing it and watching others grow and succeed is the greatest professional reward I can think of.

LEARN MORE ABOUT...

Shana O'Brien

Shana O'Brien is not only a real estate coach, but also an accredited home stager, author, educator and top-producing agent.

As the designated broker for Realty One Group Cascadia in Vancouver, Washington,, she recruits and trains some of the best and brightest real estate stars in SW Washington. Her degree in education makes her especially well-suited to the training and development of real estate agents as they progress from entry-level mentees to high-producing mega agents.

She works with her real estate clients to make the best possible decisions, whether they are buying, selling, purchasing an investment property, or considering a major remodel. Her goal is to ensure that her clients love where they live.

Originally from New Orleans, both of Shana's parents were real estate brokers and owned their own brokerage and appraisal firm.

When she's not busy coaching and managing her brokerage of 150 agents, or assisting her clients in Portland , Oregon and SW Washington, she enjoys finding vintage treasures for the mid-century home she shares with her husband and their French bulldogs.

www.ShanaOBrienRealty.com

FOCUS ON COACHING

> "When we are so busy working **in** the business, we rarely have time to work **on** the business"
>
> **CHÉRIE RONNING**

Do I Need a Business Coach?

Until the past few years, having a coach meant you played a sport. If you or your child played a sport, there was a coach. They might have been trained, or been a volunteer parent, but their job was to teach, encourage and help the team learn to play the game.

Since I have never been sports oriented, the term coach doesn't really fit my personality. For years I have called myself a mentor. I was teaching the business basics, encouraging the players and then they could "play" the game of business.

Funny thing though, is that the assumption by many was

if I was a mentor, I should be helping for free. So now I call myself an accountability and small business coach.

If you own a business or are on a career path and you feel you aren't making progress as you should, then *yes*, you need a coach.

I want to share how I work as a coach. I make no big promises of you earning six figures in thirty, sixty, or ninety days. I don't run ads that show me on a beach sipping a cocktail while the money is rolling in. Nor do I charge $997 per month to help you solve your problems.

First, we discuss what kind of help you need. Often, we don't know what we don't know. Sounds weird I know, but if your sales are down is it because you don't have a marketing plan, your website is not clear and concise, or your product may be over-priced. I start with a review of your website, and that often shows me some weaknesses and problem areas.

I don't need to know the details first; I need to know the big picture. I can help you determine the "why." In any business to be successful you need a plan. When we determine the potential problems or the "why" then we can move forward with developing a plan to solve that "why."

In all aspects of business, you need clarity on where you are headed and then develop the mindset to get there. When we are so busy working *in* the business, we rarely have time to work *on* the business. Because of that, many small business owners struggle to get things done. They fall behind in their bookkeeping, their marketing and soon they are in a mess with no way out.

But as a small business coach, I will help you make the plan, offering ideas and suggestions that work for you, your personality and your business.

Once we get a sense of order established for conquering your "why", then my accountability coaching kicks in. We create a checklist of daily and weekly tasks to get things accomplished. I check in with you every week to see what has been done and what still needs to be accomplished. After reviewing your tasks, we can decide together if the list should be revised for the upcoming week. And in working together, I become your business cheerleader!

It may take some time to clear up the first problem, and sure enough there are other problems that will rise to the surface. Business success not only requires a business plan, but so much more. You may have started your business with little of the back-office work established and now you need help to move forward efficiently and profitably. After all, this is a business, *not* a hobby!

One of the best places to get your business where you envision is to write a Business Plan—scary, right? But as a small business coach I can walk your through all of those steps to create a solid plan to move from a hobby to a real business.

A good business plan includes the following:

1. **Mission Statement**: Why you think the business is needed and what you hope to accomplish.
2. **Vision Statement**: How you see yourself accomplishing those tasks.
3. **Personal Statement**: You won't get this from the SBA—but I feel it is imperative to write your Personal Statement from the heart. Tell why you want to start the business. For example, let's say you have a dog rescue business. You are passionate about dogs, and have connections for funding, and you know that it will personally fulfill you to save these dogs and find placement for them.
4. **Operations Plan**: To include your SOP's—Standard Operating Procedures. How does the business run, who does what, and step-by-step processes for your procedures.
5. **Marketing Plan**: Which platforms you want to use, how you can do it, and how can you pay for it.
6. **Sales Plan**: Often companies call this Sales & Marketing–but these are 2 different things–what is the plan for how are you going to sell what you are marketing.

7. **Spending Plan or Budget**: Everyone hates the word budget, but since you know you are going to spend money, I call it a Spending Plan.

As part of your marketing plan, we create a content calendar for your social media. Topics for the week, month, quarter and year. These then get detailed out to your social media channels, blogs, and website.

If you are on a career path going nowhere, a personal Business Plan can be a huge help. We will work through the hierarchy of your company, your department and your skill set. Then, we construct a plan to help you advance along the career path. Maybe you are at the top of the list where you are currently employed and need to look at finding a new position with a new company, I can help.

No matter if you are a business owner or on a career path; we all face certain similar things daily. The dreaded email in-box, the To-Do list that you never shorten and consequently fall further and further behind, and the overwhelming feeling of suffocation. These are reasons you should to work with a business coach.

The dreaded email in-box in the worst. In your own business you can create different emails for customers to use, and for junk mail. Then you can focus on the important emails. At your employer's office, you may not have that capability but it is something we can research and work out.

The To-Do list—oh my! If your To-Do list is longer than a

roll of toilet paper, you are definitely in trouble! But not to worry, it can be fixed. My friend and author Alan Berg told me years ago that the "To-Do list is NOT the To-Day list." This was a total game changer for me, and for my clients. We tend to write down everything we need to do, little things along side of big projects, and the overwhelm kicks in.

My own Business Coach streamlined things for me this year with the following list:

- What is your ONE big thing you want to accomplish this year?
- Why?
- How long will it take?
- How will I accomplish it?
- Will I have fun doing it?
- What are my biggest challenges in accomplishing it?

After I answered these questions, I made a *new* To-Do list for the year, the steps to accomplish each quarter, each month, and finally, each week. This is all done in preparation to reach the ONE big thing.

The rest of the daily things should not be on a To-Do list, they should be assigned as daily or weekly tasks, and you just quickly do them and check them off. While I know this may sound overwhelming, I can make it easy for you to determine all of these things, get them set onto a calendar and then hold you accountable weekly to achieve them.

In a nutshell, a good small business or personal career coach is not only your cheerleader, but an organizer, a gentle task manager and accountability partner. It is hard work, business and careers take time, money and organization to achieve your goals.

Just like all coaches, I require an onboarding process that includes a written questionnaire from you. Once reviewed, I like to speak in person or by a zoom call to determine if we both feel like we are a good match. Everyone has different personalities and I want you to be comfortable with me.

One of my clients said I was a real "bitch", a nice one, but my coaching helped her get the work done because she knew she couldn't play me.

I am a pretty no BS person in my life and in my coaching. I will do my part and I will expect you to do yours. That way we both come out as winners.

If you don't do the assigned work prior to our check ins, being too busy is not an acceptable excuse. You are not paying me to be your friend! You are paying me to help you, to coach you, to encourage you, to offer guidance, to be your cheerleader and most of all to get you to your goals. It takes both of us to make that happen.

It is a big step to hire a coach, and it is even a bigger step to listen to the guidance they offer, and then do the work. It doesn't happen in a day or a week or even a month. My minimum requirement for coaching is three months, but six months is what most people choose. That way we can work through everything, and set solid goals and tasks, and streamline the business process.

I have been successfully self-employed for over 35 years, and still operate 2 small business today. I love what I do. I love helping you pass through the mist and clearly see where you are headed.

It is both an honor and privilege to assist each and every client along their path, and hopefully I can assist you at some point in the future.

Wishing you much success!

LEARN MORE ABOUT...

Chérie Ronning

Chérie Ronning is an international speaker, best selling author, business coach and consultant.

After over thirty years as an event planner, she transitioned into a successful speaking career and enjoys working and consulting with creative entrepreneurs.

Chérie was working at a local CPA firm (bored out of her socks), when she received a request asking if she would help plan a wedding. Chérie has always been very social and hosted many events, so she took a chance and said "Yes!" She left the CPA firm a few months later and never looked back.

The next thirty years were spent as a wedding and event planner. She opened a stationery company and founded a national networking organization for wedding professionals where she encouraged "community over competition".

Her outgoing personality, no-nonsense approach, and solid reputation naturally evolved into being asked to speak at conferences around the United States, Canada, Mexico, and Jamaica.

Chérie offers private consulting for entrepreneurs who have a great vision, but need help with business operations.

Speaking, coaching and giving back to others has kept Chérie busy and very happy!

www.cherieronning.com

> It doesn't have to be complicated to get heads turning.

NICHOLE NADKARNI

Three Steps to Business Success

Many people dream of becoming their own boss. Some of us are fortunate and were raised in an environment where entrepreneurship is modeled as easy and manageable. For others, it's something that takes some serious consideration and a huge leap of faith.

Whether you find yourself sitting bored out of your gourd at a desk job in the corporate world, or life has dealt you some challenges that require a creative mindset to fend for yourself, eventually, you'll face the decision to play it safe or go all-in on your dreams.

If you're reading this, you're either still thinking about making the big change or you've decided to commit. Either way, at some point you will wonder, "Ok. I did all the things to get started, but how do I keep this going?"

The ticket to sustaining your business is a loyal and dedicated fan. How do you create a loyal fan base?

- Slow down.
- Create an intentional, memorable experience.
- Then take a pause.
- Breathe in. Breathe out. Let it percolate.

You'll quickly know your most invested supporters, because they will be wholeheartedly sold on the value of your product or service.

A loyal, dedicated fan base doesn't have to be numerous, at least not to start. What is more important is that these people "get it." They get your mission; they can see the potential of your vision.

Even if you haven't quite fulfilled your ideal purpose, you can start by aiming to deeply fulfill your client's basic needs. Doing so will pique the interest of your future devotees.

For your marketing, create content that satisfies your audience in one or more of three categories: *educate*, *entertain*, or *inform*.

In your customer service experience, take care to understand what questions people have. Figure out how to provide answers to those questions before anyone has to ask.

When you remove obstacles in making decisions about investing in your product or service, people won't hesitate to hand over the cash.

Make sure your end-product or service absolutely delivers on what you promise. Leave no reason to question your commitment to satisfy your customer's needs.

It doesn't have to be complicated to get heads turning. Once you see prospective customers take notice, keep giving these admirers more of whatever keeps them most engaged.

As you start to convert prospects to satisfied customers, it's easy to think you've done enough (but you haven't) or get carried away in the momentum (and potentially make poor decisions).

Recognize when you're being driven by emotion. When you're running a business, there will be so many opportunities to get side tracked. Be aware of the power of fear.

Be aware of the distraction and potential excitement of shiny object syndrome. If you find yourself being driven by emotion, do not hesitate to slow down.

FOCUS ON COACHING

On the way to building or reestablishing sustainability in your business, make sure you are solid in your commitment to your mission and vision.

Make sure, if you have support staff, that everyone on the team knows the goals of the business. When things get off track, bring yourself (and team, if need be) back to your ideal outcome. Don't be afraid to examine your current state of operations.

Be honest with yourself about the health of your business. What challenges have I overcome? What challenges am continually I facing? Is my goal still relevant? Have new or better opportunities to serve my customers started to surface? Am I staying focused on developing a loyal, dedicated fan base?

One thing I suggest to business owners is establishing relevant ways to track measurability to keep you accountable. Know that you can establish metrics unique to your business and goals, and make sure you have at least one goal that tracks to profitability.

Profitability is obviously very important to the sustainability of your business, because... well, bills.

However, in the quest for maximizing profitability, whatever you do—do not lose sight of the importance of your customer experience. Put time and attention into treating your end-to-end customer delivery process as a comprehensive element of your overall product or service.

It's not just about what they get, it is also about how they got it. Be intentional. Be thorough. Everyone expects the product/service that they are coming for, but your process is where you can set yourself apart from your competition.

Theoretically, any competent competitor can deliver a similar product or service. Invite your customers to revel in the way *your* customer experience is something they can only get from *your business.*

The majority of opportunity to be more profitable that I find in my clients' businesses is somewhere along the customer service process. Look at your customer journey. What are prospects doing to find you? Once they find you, what questions will they have that need answers before they even consider putting your product in the cart or calling to set up a service consult?

Want to know one of the most obvious but under-valued things I see many businesses over look? FAQs! Figure out the Frequently Asked Questions about what you offer. You can find relevant search terms or topics by going to Google (then look for the "related search terms" for more ideas). Look up the FAQs on sites of industry leaders in your market or larger metropolitan markets. Drop these questions in a document. Then start brain dumping *YOUR* answers to these questions.

There are so many things you can do with this information once you have it noted in your own terms!

FOCUS ON COACHING

(That's another chapter in another book, but for the love of all the stars in the night sky... have answers to these questions.) Also, your customers will contact you with plenty of questions themselves (even if you have these answers posted online and written on printed materials).

Write down what people inquire about. By gathering this information, you're prepared to remove the "investment obstacle" as quickly as it arises.

If you're not sold that attention to detail in your customer service experience is invaluable, think about a time when you got what you wanted, but the process in getting the thing was fraught with friction.

Next, think about a time when you got what you wanted, but actually, you got so much *more*. Which experience made you want to go back and support that business again? Be the business you'd want to go back to.

There are so many ways to surprise and delight. Start with the simple stuff, then over time add more layers of intent and thoroughness to your end-to-end experience until your customers have no reason to consider their needs could be better met elsewhere.

Once you've done the work to create a memorable experience, take a moment to pause. After you've delivered what you've promised, it's up to the customer to internalize whether or not you took care in meeting their expectations. This happens organically.

If you delivered a regular or below expectations experience, your customer may still be satisfied. However, if that's all you did, your business may have missed a great opportunity to create a raving fan that will sing your praises.

You can't pay for genuine word-of-mouth advertising; it is a result that comes from the work you put into creating that super satisfying memorable experience.

While doing relationship management after you deliver your product or service can never hurt, customers who are truly impressed are highly likely to invite themselves back to your business on their own. They are also more likely to recruit new prospects into your pipeline.

If you can, find a way to reward those happy customers who recruit on your behalf. If you do, use rewards that are actually valuable to the customer, not just beneficial to your business.

Stay anchored in your mission and vision, make the effort to commit to giving great customer service, and allow your customers to sell themselves into coming back for more and you won't have to worry about how to stay in business.

LEARN MORE ABOUT...

Nichole Nadkarni

Based out of San Francisco, Nichole Nadkarni is the Chief Solution Wizard at Red Fish Viral.

While business owners are focused on the details of daily operations, she sees the whole galaxy of untapped potential.

Guiding businesses to thrive by developing intentional, memorable experiences is just one of the many ways she leads businesses to make industry competitors irrelevant.

Connect with Nichole at nichole@redfishviral.com

www.redfishviral.com

Look for upcoming books in our
Focus On...series.
An exciting new book series created for entrepreneurs.

Learn new strategies, develop expertise, increase knowledge and grow your business!

It's time to share your story.

We're here to help you,
every step of the way.

hello@gallivantpress.com
www.gallivantpress.com

www.ingramcontent.com/pod-product-compliance
Lightning Source LLC
Chambersburg PA
CBHW050324120526
44592CB00014B/2037